Pure Curry

Unique Jazz Settings
of Favorite Hymns
by Craig Curry

CONTENTS

Foreword

If you are not familiar with jazz harmonies, this collection will hopefully whet your appetite for more! For many classically trained pianists, jazz is something of a mystery. My hope is that these arrangements will have you sounding like a "jazzer" in no time. As with my other piano collections, I offer fully notated "improvised" solos right in the arrangements. Those with a jazz background may feel free to improvise their own. Chord symbols are included to help in this regard or as a tool for analyzing the harmonies.

When you're looking for something a little "different," be it for your own enjoyment at home or for worship or recital, I hope you'll find these arrangements just the thing. God bless you as you serve Him at the piano!

Sincerely,

Craig Curry
www.craigcurry.com

Craig Curry is a highly regarded free-lance composer and arranger. Described as "one of the freshest musical voices around," he is the recipient of numerous ASCAP awards and was the winner of the Fanny Crosby Choral Composition Competition. He is widely published and holds degrees from Wheaton College and the University of Miami. Passionate about worship, Craig served for 12 years as a worship pastor in Wichita, Kansas where he lives with his wife and two children.

I Must Tell Jesus

I believe the bluesy and emphatic nature of this arrangement fits this hymn quite well. Are the blues the modern equivalent of the psalms of lament? I think so. "I must tell Jesus all of my trials, I cannot bear these burdens alone." Dedicated to a retired Wheaton College professor, Clayton Halvorsen, under whose direction I spent four wonderful years in a male choir. He always enjoyed creative church music. I can still hear his voice and picture the twinkle in his eyes as he used to say, "Please hold on while the sanctuary is in motion."

Rock of Ages

I admit it, this one is a play on words. But don't you think a song called "Rock of Ages" should, well, rock? Just a little? Dedicated to the Senior Pastor of Wichita First Baptist Church, Dan Hawn, and his wife Sally. Dan likes to rock.

This Is My Father's World

A more introspective treatment than one usually hears of this hymn. Lots of jazz harmonies in here though. Dedicated to a dear college friend, Teresa Anstatt.

Love Divine, All Loves Excelling

This one is a peppy little samba. Try to keep the time absolutely steady, with an accent on the second half of the beat, as is the case with Brazilian music. Dedicated to my brother-in-law and his family.

Rejoice, the Lord Is King!

One doesn't usually hear this hymn in three, let alone as a jazz waltz, but I think it suits it well. The key to making this one shine is by paying close attention to the sudden dynamic changes. Dedicated to my good friend and my former piano professor, Dr. William Phemister, Chair of the Piano Department at Wheaton College.

Near to the Heart of God
There may be some Duke Ellington influences floating around this arrangement. If it's too hard, you're playing it too fast. Take it nice and slow and feel free to play with the tempo by using rubato. Dedicated to my children, Ella and Cole. Every Christian father's prayer for his kids is that they would be near to God's heart.

Thou Art Worthy
What happens if you take this song a faster tempo than usual? It becomes a bossa nova! I wouldn't necessarily recommend singing it with this breezy style, but I think as an instrumental solo it fits nicely. Dedicated to my church's Office Manager, Lesa Gardner and her husband, Jim.

Wonderful Words of Life
This arrangement is the most adventurous harmonically, but its slow tempo should help you as you reach for those different sounding chords. I've found that when I slow down many of the old bouncy gospel hymns, I discover a lovely melody and a very meaningful text. You can use lots of rubato on this one, but it will work at a slightly faster tempo also. Dedicated to my church's Director of Missions, TJ Akin.

For the Beauty of the Earth
As I worked on this arrangement I focused on the beautiful and majestic sounds the piano is capable of making. This is mainly heard in the rhapsodic interlude in the middle of the piece, a storm that eventually gives way to a calm ending. Dedicated to a college buddy of mine, Scott Johnson, who serves with Youth for Christ in Beirut, Lebanon.

Joyful, Joyful, We Adore Thee
The opening rhythmic pattern is called a "montuno," one of the characteristic sounds of Afro-Cuban music or Latin jazz. This arrangement should not be played "pretty." Attack! For those who are familiar with Latin music, this arrangement follows a 2-3 clavéé. Dedicated to a former colleague and his wife, Lyn and Julie Perry.

for Clayton Halvorsen

I MUST TELL JESUS

ELISHA A. HOFFMAN
Arranged by CRAIG CURRY

for Dan and Sally Hawn

ROCK OF AGES

THOMAS HASTINGS
Arranged by CRAIG CURRY

Driving gospel rock feel (♩ = 140)
Straight 8th notes

for Teresa Anstatt

THIS IS MY FATHER'S WORLD

Traditional English melody
Arranged by CRAIG CURRY

24

for Tim, Becky, Heather and Brandon Whaley

LOVE DIVINE, ALL LOVES EXCELLING

JOHN ZUNDEL
Arranged by CRAIG CURRY

30

for Bill Phemister

REJOICE, THE LORD IS KING!

JOHN DARWALL
Arranged by CRAIG CURRY

38

for Ella and Cole

NEAR TO THE HEART OF GOD

CLELAND B. McAFEE
Arranged by CRAIG CURRY

for Jim and Lesa Gardner

THOU ART WORTHY

PAULINE M. MILLS
Arranged by CRAIG CURRY

for TJ Akin

WONDERFUL WORDS OF LIFE

PHILIP P. BLISS
Arranged by CRAIG CURRY

for Scott Johnson

FOR THE BEAUTY OF THE EARTH

CONRAD KOCHER
Arranged by CRAIG CURRY

for Lyndon and Julie Perry

JOYFUL, JOYFUL, WE ADORE THEE

LUDWIG VAN BEETHOVEN
Arranged by CRAIG CURRY